Mother Duck
and
Baby Crow

by Catherine Depp
Illustrated by Judith Pfeiffer

Editorial Offices: Glenview, Illinois • Parsippany, New Jersey • New York, New York
Sales Offices: Needham, Massachusetts • Duluth, Georgia • Glenview, Illinois
Coppell, Texas • Sacramento, California • Mesa, Arizona

It is a windy and rainy day.
Mother Duck and her ducklings
cannot go outside.
They hear a loud noise.

2

crow

door

step

What could it be?
Did a branch fall?
Mother Duck opens the door.
A baby crow is on her step.

"Are you hurt?" Mother Duck asks.
"No, Mrs. Duck," says Baby Crow.
"The wind blew very hard.
It blew me out of the nest."

"I'm so sorry," says Mother Duck.
"You should come inside with us.
We'll have warm tea and bread.
After the storm, we will look for
your parents."

The storm has ended.
There is a knock on the door.
It is Mr. and Mrs. Crow.
They are looking for their baby.

"Please come in," says Mrs. Duck.
Mr. and Mrs. Crow look very happy.
Baby Crow is safe and warm.
"Thank you for helping Baby Crow,
good neighbor!" says Mrs. Crow.

Father Crow says, "We will be good
friends now."
"It is nice to have good friends," says
Mrs. Duck.
"How very nice!"

Talk About It

1. Tell what happens in the story from the beginning to the end.
2. If the ducklings ever needed help, do you think Mr. and Mrs. Crow would help them?

Write About It

3. Which part of this story did you like the best? On a sheet of paper, draw a picture of that part of the story. Write about the animals in your drawing.

Extend Language

Cold and *strong* are two words which tell about the wind.
The wind is *cold*. The wind is *strong*.
Do you know any other words to tell about the wind?

ISBN: 0-328-14122-4

5 6 7 8 9 10 V3FL 14 13 12 11 10 09

ELL Reader

Genre	Build Background	Access Content	Extend Language
Fantasy	• **Problem Solving** • **Citizenship** • **Helping Others**	• **Labels in Pictures** • **Questions in Text**	• **Adjectives for the Wind**

Scott Foresman Reading Street 1.5.2

PEARSON

Scott Foresman

scottforesman.com

ISBN 0-328-14122-4

90000

9 780328 141227

Economic Benefits of Improved Water Quality: Public Perceptions of Option and Preservation Values

Douglas A. Greenley,
Richard G. Walsh, and Robert A. Young

Studies in Water Policy and Management, No. 3

Westview Press